THE RAFT OF THE MEDUSA

THE RAFT OF THE MEDUSA

Five Voices on Colonies, Nations and Histories

edited by
Jocelyne Doray and Julian Samuel

commentaries by
Charles Acland, Will Straw and Marvan Hassan

**BLACK
ROSE
BOOKS**

**Montréal/New York
London**

BLACK ROSE BOOKS No. W198
Hardcover ISBN 1-895431-77-8
Paperback ISBN 1-895431-76-X

Library of Congress No. 93-72751

Canadian Cataloguing in Publication Data

The Raft of the Medusa: five voices on colonies, nations and histories

Includes bibliographical references.
ISBN: 1-895431-77-8 (bound)
ISBN: 1-985431-76-X (pbk.)

1. History—Philosophy. 2. Historiography. I. Doray, Jocelyne, 1955- .
II. Samuel, Julian

D13.2.R33 1993   901   C93-090487-7

Book design and layout: Nat Klym
Cover design: Nat Klym and Julian Samuel
Cover Illustration: Detail from *The Raft of the Medusa*, by Julian Samuel, 1993.
Front page: Detail from *Le radeau de la Méduse*, Salon de 1819, by Géricault.

Mailing Address

BLACK ROSE BOOKS
C.P. 1258
Succ. Place du Parc
Montréal, Québec
H2W 2R3 Canada

BLACK ROSE BOOKS
340 Nagel Drive
Cheektowaga, New York
14225 USA

Printed in Canada
A publication of the Institute of Policy Alternatives of Montréal (IPAM)

CONTENTS

1.

THE RAFT OF THE MEDUSA

Five Voices on Colonies, Nations and Histories

a video documentary
by Julian Samuel

interviews with:
Ackbar Abbas
Thierry Hentsch
Amin Maalouf
M. Nourbese Philip
Sara Suleri

First Citizen; "... If the wars eat us
not up, they will; and there's all
the love they bear us."

Coriolanus,
William Shakespeare

This isn't the dawn we waited for.

"Dawn of Freedom,"
(August 1947)
Faiz Ahmed Faiz

SUMMARY EXECUTION UNDER THE MOORISH KINGS OF GRANADA

HENRY RENAULT, 1870

Amin Maalouf

History has too often been told from a Eurocentric point of view: the world is interpreted by
Europe in a way which conforms to Europe's
interests, and, I would say, to Europe's concerns. This is true at every level, including the
geographical perspective in the world.

I think that the world can be seen and narrated
from many different positions. And I think that
each vision of the world, each point of view, is
important.

Thierry Hentsch

History is always written according to the preoccupations of the moment, and according to
preoccupations of those who fabricate history,
who write it today and who have written it in the
past.

However, today we may tend to consider a certain number of phenomena which were left behind in the past. It is clear that Marx played a
fundamental role in this way of looking at history. It is also clear that through this vision of
history, our way of considering other cultures
has also changed.

M. Nourbese Philip

The expression "conventional history" becomes almost synonymous with European history.

I see that very much as a thing apart, in many respects, from Black history. But Black history is inserted into conventional history in very problematic ways, firstly because, for someone like myself coming from a colonial society, the history that we were taught in schools was European history, and it was a very conventional approach to history.

We, Black peoples, really only came upon ourselves in history as objects upon which the European had carried out his various projects. We never really saw ourselves as agents in history. We, African peoples in the New World, and even in Africa, were told clearly that we did not have a history.

So it has been almost a lifelong project to excavate our histories. I use that in the plural and with a small "h" vis-à-vis the larger history.

I see my role as subverting European history by positioning ourselves as agents, within the period of history capital "H." We have always been there in that history. However, we have been written out, silenced, left on the margins. In terms of my writing life, I continually try to reverse that: to position ourselves as centre and not merely as the object upon which the European has acted.

Julian Samuel

Would there exist such configurations as Third World Nation-States without the Atlantic European, the Empires indirectly freeing-up a potential for national self-definition?

Sara Suleri

Well, you are asking the question of the hour aren't you really?

With what I would call the crumbling of the Nation-State in the West, we have had to requestion the ways in which nationalisms were transplanted to the so-called Third World. I would say that in some ways, of course there were indigenous local nationalisms that grew out of, lets say, the Indian subcontinent in the nineteenth century. So we cannot merely see the nation as the product of the West.

Nourbese Philip,
writer/critic

Julian Samuel

What exactly happened on midnight August 14th, 1947?

Sara Suleri

To my mind a very sad thing happened in midnight August 14th. I think it is best emblematized by the fact that when India was partitioned, they messed it up. Pakistan got independence on the 14th and India got independence on the 15th, and what was the status of India during that period of twenty-four hours? Was it a nation? Was it a colony?

What we see in the Partition of India was the great mistake whereby Mohammed Ali Jinnah assumed that he could use religion in order to produce a modern secular State. And I think that for Pakistan, the great tragedy was that Jinnah did not live long enough. If he had lived long enough to write a secular constitution, they would never have dreamt of changing a word of the Quaids constitution. As a consequence, Pakistan would still be a secular country today.

Julian Samuel

Can you tell me what Hong Kong was before it became an important capital?

Ackbar Abbas

Before the British, it was just a piece of rock. It was a just a fishing village. Of course, you had the British presence, but one of the crucial changes was 1949: after '49, the key event in the development of Hong Kong was this influx of talent from China, all the way from cooks to tailors to entrepreneurs. All the people who, for whatever reason, wanted out of China came to Hong Kong. It was a kind of hot house atmosphere and it developed that way.

Julian Samuel

Does Hong Kong fit into any previous Asian situations? Or is Hong Kong's relationship to international capital a unique one?

Ackbar Abbas

The question of a time gap really has to be part of the equation. Things did not develop in a linear, chronological way.

Sara Suleri,
writer/critic

In some ways of course its not unique. You could think about it as a Third World country, and all the discourses on the Third World would, to a certain extent, apply. But because of both the history and the geography, and because of its relationship to the West and to China, you have something else that is happening: you have almost a break in logic and time, and space.

On the one hand it has always been in this position of dependency, for water or for whatever, either on the West or on China. But at the same time, it has also been able to develop in a very quick way. So what you are then getting is a gap. The word that I would use here is "hysteresis," in the sense that the distance between cause and effect is a long one.

So is it unique? I think, in one sense, it is a very unique situation, especially if you think of what is going to happen after 1997. As I see it, one of the things that is going to happen after '97, when Hong Kong is going to pass from Britain to China, is that it will keep its status, in a sense, as a colony. But it is going to a be a colony of China, in a peculiar way. It is not going to be a colony in a dependent subaltern position. In some ways, it is in a much more advanced position than the country colonizing it. So, it becomes a specific form of post-coloniality, in the specific sense of the word: the postcolonial has not yet gone through a process of decolonization. And I think that this is historically unique about Hong Kong and the Hong Kong situation.

Amin Maalouf

I think it is important to know world history, and to know the reality of the world from many different points of view. It is only from these different points of view that one can have an idea anywhere close to reality. From our daily standpoint we have too often a picture of history, a picture of geography, such that, for example, a region like the one we call the Near East, which is the birthplace of some of the greatest civilizations, the birthplace of history, is called today the Near East. In other words, it is defined solely by the distance that separates it from Europe.

For me, this habit is aberrant and scandalous, and also dangerous. Today, if we don't come to see the world, and its history, and its present, from a very large number of different points of

view, then it means that we are going against
something fundamental.

Perhaps I will elaborate on this question. I think
that there is, in Europe today — I say Europe
but it is not only Europe, it is both Europe and
North America, the whole centre of civilization
of European origin which is the most advanced
civilization today — we have then, in the Occident, the only civilization with a universal vocation and pretension. All the other civilizations
appear as marginal ones.

This civilization with a universal vocation is, for
all sorts of technical reasons and others, in the
process of becoming a civilization extended
over the entire world: its values, its ways of
living, its habits of consumption, are spreading.

If this civilization does not assume a true
universality, there is a conflict that cannot help
but be aggravated between this civilization and
all marginal civilizations that consider it as a
foreign one. It has to state outright: I have a
vocation, I have a universal ambition, therefore
I must become universal, that is to say I have to
behave not like a civilization planted in a particular geographical location, at the scene of
one civilization, but truly consider that I have to

Amin Maalouf,
writer.

become universal, that I have to integrate external relations, that I have to integrate different visions.

What I tried to do through *The Crusades Through Arab Eyes*, and in a slightly different manner in other books, was firstly to address myself to this civilization saying: You cannot continue to see the world as you saw it two or three centuries ago. You cannot continue to name regions of the world, even if it has no more than a symbolic value, in the same way that you named them before.

When Christopher Columbus sets off towards India, and he comes by mistake across a continent which is not India, that he calls the inhabitants of this continent Indians, that's understandable. But if five centuries later we continue to call them American Indians, there is something fundamentally unhealthy in this way of permanently interpreting the world, with an utterly clear conscience, as if the rest of the world was simply a distant, marginal periphery, without real importance save to the extent that it has relations with Europe.

There are more and more conflicts which, as I see it, have their roots in the rejection by a great number of different cultures, by a great number of different peoples. European culture is in full expansion, and it gives rise to reactions of defense. These reactions do nothing but increase, and they will continue to increase as long as this culture remains so strictly Eurocentric.

Thierry Hentsch

I think that our way of viewing history as well as our way of constructing a novel, for instance, is influenced by both Marx and Freud. Take for example Proust's *Remembrance of Things Past* which is ultimately the history of an individual within a particular society; it may have inspired historians, but it has also been inspired by other trends, among which is the psycho-analytical trend, I believe, even if this was a unconscious move on the part of the author.

A way of depicting the Orient as despotic and fanatic, among other things, is part of an imaginaire which has been constructed in the West, by opposition to a vision which the West wanted to have of itself.

The Orient is a mirror in which the West sees its image, but a reversed image. And in this mirror,

the West constructed its own image, a self-image. This has been possible because the Orient — particularly this part of the Orient which is near, geographically, and which was, historically, close to the West for a long period of time — this "Near Orient" has been the perfect "other" by which the West positioned itself, perhaps even more so now that the soviet threat has come to an end.

This "other" need be as different as possible, on as many grounds as possible, to "us."

If "we" have democracy, the "other," by opposition, has despotism and tyranny. If "we" have tolerance, the "other" has fanaticism, etc. It works through binarism.

But in reality, this way of viewing the Orient has been tremendously harmful to East/West relations. It has also been harmful to the development of the thought and of the society in the Arab-Moslem Mediterranean, or, shall I say, the Mediterranean Orient.

It has been harmful in two ways: on material grounds, of course, because the Western colonies, penetrating these societies, have disrupted them, transformed them, and also destabilized them. At the same time, they have hindered the reflection that these societies would have had upon their own history, because this interruption has, in a sense, forced the people, the intellectuals of these countries, to think their own history not only through the history of the West, but through a perspective with which the West viewed its own history.

We can view the history of the West according to a number of different viewpoints. The West has its own point of view. But the people who have been, or still are under Western domination have a different perspective.

Julian Samuel

What are national literary allegories?

Sara Suleri

They are texts that purport to tell a national history via a fictional form. The clearest example that I could give you would of course be Midnight's Children, which was the story of both the birth of a nation, and the birth of a nation being absolutely parallel with the life of the protagonist of the novel. So, you have a character that represents India, as well as himself, and you have Indian national history told from his perspective.

I believe colonialism initiates nationhood by its very advent, so that for example, we look at the British Raj, and try to say: When did the nationalist movement in India start? We would have to date it from 1857, from the moment of mutiny. So that in some ways, the colonial experience is automatically modernizing. It makes the colonized people modern even before their time.

M. Nourbese Philip

Surely when we are celebrating Emancipation Day, we are colluding with the European in eliding, in erasing a long history of resistance, of rebellion that made slave societies continuously very tense. Slave owners, slave masters could never be sure of what would happen or what would not happen.

Emancipation Day suggests that somehow the European could give us something of our freedom. And while, yes, it did have tremendous power in that Africans could, for the first time, do certain things that they could not do before, it in no way affected what they always knew — that they were always human.

I think that it is very important to look at that history in a very questioning way and that we continually try to subvert it. Even for an event like Emancipation Day.

In fact when you look at slave societies, you look at African societies in the New World, and you see the tremendous production of creativity, in the face of a traumatic onslaught. You look at the music, you look at the dancing and so on that continues right up to today, which were produced under terrible circumstances, and all of it is, in itself, a testament to the fact that the European could not, by a paper document, take away from us our essential humanity.

We knew our spirituality was still intact even though it was under attack. We knew our music was there. The Caribbean demotic is as much a descendent of African tongues as it is of English.

So, what I'm saying, in fact, is that the people who should be celebrating Emancipation Day are actually the Europeans, since it represents, for them, progress — they finally understood that there was something wrong — something unacceptable in holding people as property, as slaves.

Amin Maalouf

I think that Europe's attitude towards the rest of the world is a conquering attitude, an attitude that, over the centuries, has had effects which were sometimes positive and sometimes negative, but always devastating.

Sometimes Europe has transmitted its culture to the world, often at an extremely high price. One sees what Europe did in Africa, in the American continent, the massacre of American Indians, the transport of millions of Africans by whole shiploads to America, to make them work in the place of Indians who were massacred, the war fought with China to force them to buy opium, all sorts of conflict that scarred the people they came in contact with.

I see in Europe a total incomprehension to the sometimes very violent reactions of certain peoples in relation to Europe.

One has the impression, in Europe, of being unjustly accused of something. People have no memory. It is true that, when one looks at the

surface of things, it is difficult to side with an Algerian who reacts very violently against a Frenchman who is a perfect democrat, who looks upon Algeria with a smile and possibly with a lot of sympathy.

When one looks at the historical evolution, when one takes into account that there were 130 years of French occupation in Algeria, that there were massacres, that there was the destruction of one culture in the name of imposing another, for a people who continue to live in a state of genuine frustration, who still do not succeed in escaping from these years, from this century of tragedy, who are still seeking their identity, it is not as simple as it is for a people who are prosperous and developed.

And the explosions of violence that we can see in certain countries are often the slightly delayed reactions to another violence that was imposed on the people who have forgotten today that they were violent. And sometimes it is good to remind them. Not particularly to make them feel guilty, but because I think there is a fundamental misunderstanding, and this is more specific to Europe and the Islamic world.

Europe does not know Islam any better now than it did a thousand years ago. I think that essentially, it is satisfied with a small number of general ideas, sometimes a little correct, often very false, that are spread at any given moment, that everyone accepts as they are. There is a sort of moral terror, of intellectual terror such that there is a fixed number of ideas which one cannot challenge. And there can be conflicts, massacres, hatreds that develop, without people really making an effort to know the "other" better.

M. Nourbese Philip

Postmodernism suggests that history is dead, and I take issue with that. As a Black person in the new world, history is not dead for me. History is very much alive, particularly coming from the Caribbean which represents for me a site of vast interruptions of "histories."

It was a site of interruption of the aboriginal peoples, an interruption of their history, their "circuits" of creativity and culture. You then have the interruption of the African history, their histories, their "circuits" bringing them into the New World. You have an interruption of European history with the advent of the European thinking that he was going to find Utopia, the New World where none of the sins of the Old World would exist. You also have the interruption of the Asian history with the coming of the Chinese and Indians.

So the legacies of these histories and their impact on the people of the Caribbean and the New World are very much with us today, so how can history be dead?

Julian Samuel

Are there any historians who are making a case for the political/historical freezing of Third World societies because they have been held in check by the expansions of Western economies? I know you have previously answered the question, sort of, but are there any precise detailings of the anti-liberalism, let us say, in the Algerian case now: one could say that initially the Algerian revolution was part of a modernity which was French installed — or somehow was dialectically constructed with French imperialism there. Are there any historians that are making the case for this "de-modernity," this "anti-modernity?"

Thierry Hentsch

The question is: Who do the historians render responsible for this situation — is the West responsible for it, or else, is the "other," the Orient, responsible for it?

I think that most Western historians blame this immobility, this incapacity of entering modernization, on the Orient. To start with, Marx's vision of these problems is extremely Eurocentric. When he talks of the Asiatic mode of production, or when he talks of Asia as a whole, he describes these societies as stalled societies in which the intervention of capitalism, coming from the outside, is like "a stick in an ant's nest," forcing these societies to evolve, to transform themselves, and to enter the course of history.

Marx makes an apology for colonization, in spite of its horrors — and Marx talks at length about these horrors — but he says: colonization is necessary despite its horrors, because it is the impetus for these countries to reenter the course of history, or what we, Westerners, consider as the course of history. I would call it a Hegelian vision of history, which Marx adopted totally. I think that in the nineteenth century, the particularity of this Western vision of the Orient is that it is somehow linked to death.

Julian Samuel

Isn't it a bit dramatic?

Thierry Hentsch

Indeed, it is dramatic … Linked to death in all senses of the word. I mean, the Orient is stalled. It is dead. It does not evolve. At the same time, the Orient is a kind of thereafter. It is another world. It is not our world. It is a world, now viewed in a more positive way, of dreams, where it is possible to escape.

We may not forget that nineteenth century Europe acknowledged the bewilderment and the ugliness of the industrial revolution. Thereafter, the Orient, which has not yet entered the cycle of the industrial hideousness, remains a dreamland. And it is in this sense that this world is, altogether, a dead one. Dead. The thereafter. Something radically different, viewed from the other side of a fence.

And so, of course, what moves, what lives, what evolves is sited at home, in the West.

But, dead, also, because there is a link made with despotism, fanaticism and bloodshed. One of the most representative paintings depicting this Western way of thinking is *The Death of Sardanapalus,* by Eugène Delacroix.

Sara Suleri

Cultures yoked by violence together. The phrase is in fact Dr. Johnson's and he is, in the original context, talking about the metaphysical poets.

However, I use it to talk about the fact that in pre-partition India, the cultures yoked by violence together are of course the Hindu culture, the Moslem culture, and the growing Christian culture that was present with the colonizer. And none of these people really wanted one another.

Thierry Hentsch

Why did Marxism regain a certain popularity and fervour in the universities during the sixties? Well, to me, it seems directly linked to the rise of grievances within the ex-colonized countries, and also to the critique of the injustices produced by the world order. This critique was not only academic: it was also taking place in different political arenas and other forums. Therefore, this interest in Marxism was linked to

THE DEATH OF
SARDANAPALUS,
1829
EUGÈNE DELACROIX
fanaticism, and bloodshed.

THE NUBIAN GUARD,
(BEFORE OR AFTER
THE PARIS COMMUNE
OF 1871)
LUDWIG DEUTSCH

the rise of the Third World as a force of revindication.

But today, it is clear that the Third World has not succeeded in bettering its relations with the First World, or let's say the capitalist developed world. There was a certain disillusionment with Third World regimes which claimed to have a progressive vision of history, because they failed to install, within their borders, egalitarian societies.

Therefore, nowadays, in the universities, there is a depreciation of the Third World and the problems it poses, simply because it is in a weaker position today, politically and ideologically, than fifteen or twenty years ago. I think that it is a particularity of Western society to have a bad conscience of its imperialism.

But let's be careful. It is a bad conscience expressed by a minority which usually is not in power. When it comes to power, as with the socialists in France, this bad conscience tends to vanish. So, it is a bad conscience which tends to circulate, more or less, according to the moment, among intellectuals. And I think, though I may be wrong, that this bad conscience is a typically Western phenomenon. I doubt that the Chinese ever had second thoughts about exerting hegemony around them. I doubt that the Ottomans ever had these preoccupations, or the Mongols, or the Romans, or Alexander.

Ackbar Abbas

In a sense, Hong Kong has had no history. There is nothing to exhume but all these traces and residues of the colonial, that in fact is your history. So, you cannot get outside this colonial situation. Before the British, Hong Kong was just this barren rock, so the whole history of Hong Kong is the history of the colonial presence.

There has never been "a before." It has always been what it is.

It is like the question of language of speaking. One of the resistance strategies might be to say, all right, I don't want to speak English. I'm going to speak Chinese. But that's no good either. When you do that, as it were, when you choose another language, that is also a kind of cop out. A better way to do it would be to speak English in such a way that it has never been spoken before. Use it, but in a different way. Put a kind of spin on it.

M. Nourbese Philip

My central preoccupation as a writer comes out of language, and how I, as someone whose ancestors were stripped of their languages, function in a tongue which is both mother and father tongue.

When we think of mother tongue, we think of all the connotations that come along with the word "mother": warmth, softness, nurturing and so on.

But the English language in the Caribbean, in the New World, was not mothering in that sense. If it was at all, it was m/othering. This was a language that was forced on individuals. People only heard it in the most debased of situations, orders, commands, that sort of thing. But yet the people, the peoples were versatile, were resilient enough to combine the leavings of that language along with what they remembered from their own languages, to create what I think is one of the most exciting and kinetic vernaculars in the English speaking world today: the Caribbean demotic, which some people call patois or dialect.

Amin Maalouf

I think that all the conflicts that have taken place over the last millennium between the Christian Occident and the Moslem world have given rise to certain references to the crusades, from both sides. The crusades remain the most important conflict for these two worlds.

In Europe today, one has the impression that those who refer incorrectly to the crusades are the Moslems, and that Europe has long over-come this whole question. I would say this is partly true and partly false.

It's partly false, first, because I feel often in the attitude of many Europeans, a visceral distrust towards Islam. It is not always conscious, it is rarely admitted, but it is real. I think that it will be a long time before a Moslem country is accepted into the European Community. I know that, for example, the Turks have expressed a desire to be in the EEC. I would be very surprised if this works. There are certainly economic, demographic or other reasons, but I am fundamentally convinced that the religious reason is primary.

Somewhere, even though people do not always use religious references, in their mind,

Islam appears — today more than before — as an enemy. With the disappearance of the communist danger, it is in fact perhaps even becoming, for many people in Occidental Europe, the replacement, enemy number one.

Julian Samuel

How is the practice of Islam in Europe different from that which is practiced in Pakistan?

Sara Suleri

It is very different and it has much to do with class. So, I will have to answer this question in a couple of parts. If you're talking about the working class that practices Islam, they are probably more ridged. They believe even more tenaciously than your typical village in Pakistan, where religion is practised, but is not necessarily associated with fanaticism.

I believe that sometimes immigration exacerbates the problems of fundamentalism. They are alone, they are a minority, they are in a country that does not really want them, and that is what produces the mentality of the Bradford Moslems who want book burning and much more. Whereas, if you return to the middle class situation in Pakistan and Britain, it is the opposite mirror image. This typical Pakistan middle class is far more religious than the equivalent here.

So, indeed, Islam is very very different in the West.

Thierry Hentsch

The industrial revolution, and all the technical changes that go with it, and the particular power that it gives to the West, radically transforms its relations with the Orient in a practically irreversible way.

The Orient is no longer viewed as an equal but as an inferior. Whereas before, this inferiority — let's talk about economic inferiority — was not obvious. For a long time, in the trade relations, the European countries were in debt, and the Ottoman Empire was in surplus, even until the beginning of the nineteenth century.

It is not obvious that towards the end of the eighteenth century, and even during the seventeenth century, the Europeans have had a clear notion of their own economic superiority. Perhaps they already had a notion of their scientific superiority: Some authors of this era comment that the Easterners are very knowledgeable but they lack "our great modern methods." So there is already this notion that the Orient is left behind.

But it is not behind economically speaking. This idea of economic backwardness which gave way to the idea of underdevelopment, is deeply anchored in the nineteenth century and is obviously linked to the economic power of the industrial revolution, and of Western industry at large.

M. Nourbese Philip

David Livingstone was in his own words very clear about the fact that he had to destroy African culture. While he expressed respect for it on many occasions, he was also very clear that he had to destroy African culture — their mores, their customs. Then he could bring commerce to them, and Christianity …

Julian Samuel

Did he not want to bring Christianity first?

M. Nourbese Philip

No. He was very clear about this: commerce, then Christianity. I'm familiar with this because in completing a book recently, I had cause to do fairly extensive research on him.

Very much the myth of Livingstone is that he went to Africa and brought religion, and helped to end the slave trade. Livingstone had one convert in all his life as a missionary chief of the Bangwedo. And shortly after Livingstone converted him, this man returned to his native spirituality and religion.

So Livingstone as missionary was an utter and absolute failure.

Sara Suleri

I feel very strongly that we pay too much attention to disempowerment of the colonial situation without also realising that to be a colonizer is not the simplest thing in the world. There is an inherent powerlessness in the situation and that is what increases this sense of the anxiety of Empire. So that the standard colonizer was a very anxious person and that is a kind of dynamic of powerlessness between colonizer/ colonized that I wished to discuss in my book.

Julian Samuel

Why did you choose Livingstone as a source for your book?

M. Nourbese Philip

The best way of answering that is to say that in a way I am using Livingstone as a concept: Livingstone chose me to present an alternative view of history. That book was actually a reply to the book I have mentioned earlier, called, *She Tries Her Tongue, Her Silence Softly Breaks,* in which I examined language.

I immersed myself totally in language. The terror that language has meant for certain peoples in this world. And I am speaking about Africans in the New World. The terror and terrorism of language.

At the end of that work, I felt myself confronted by the concept of silence — what was it? was it always negative? and so on. I began writing a long poem looking into this concept, and felt that the poem was becoming too intense. And so I began to break it up, which was in keeping with the earlier work which also worked with interruptions.

Livingstone is also working along that form of interruptions, but somehow Livingstone the man presented himself to me as the symbol of silence: the silencer, as in the European who goes overseas or to North America, to South America, to Australia, to Africa and finds a world there, but then imposes his silence on the peoples forcing his tongue, literally, on them.

Julian Samuel

Is it possible to connect to the anxious colonizer with emergent nationalism and terror?

Sara Suleri

That's a very interesting proposition. And if we wanted to pursue the analogy we would have to talk about issues of degree because anxiety and terror are not part of the same spectrum. I think that in some ways, psychically speaking, anxiety is just as corrosive as living with terror. But the world of terrorism is far more literally and immediately dangerous to one.

Now when you talk about the relation of terror to emergent nationalism, I assume you mean the ways in which countries are prepared to kill in order to emerge? Is that your point?

Amin Maalouf

From the Arab point of view, things are always seen a little through the influence of the crusades. It is linked to the fact, I think, that in the Arab world there is still not a true separation between the past and the present.

In the history of a people, there are moments of rupture that allow them to identify with an event, a period, an epoch, and to trace their roots from this epoch.

The French Revolution is a period of rupture. A Frenchman doesn't feel the need to refer to any period previous to the French Revolution. It is sufficient for him to consider that he belongs to a world that was forged by the French Revolution.

There is an even more recent reference, which is the liberation in 1945. I think there are even many people who do not feel it necessary to refer to an earlier period. More generally, in the Occidental world, people feel good: they have sufficient references, they have something that flatters their identity.

For the Arabs, this is not the case. This is not true solely for the Arabs, but particularly for the

Arabs. For them, there is nothing in the world today that can comfort them in their identity, nothing to be proud of. They have to go far back into the past, to when they were the dominant civilization: if we talk of sciences, they cannot refer to Arab science today, because it does not exist. They have to go back to Avicenna or Berunii.

In any case, in the realm of the scientific or cultural, and military, we cannot refer to recent victories because they do not exist. When one thinks of a victory, one thinks of Saladin, one thinks of the crusades because it is the last great victory in the confrontation with the Occident. One cannot ask an Arab — and for me this is something fundamental — one cannot ask an Arab, a Moslem, to bury the past. At that moment it cannot be separated from a fundamental element of his identity.

He could start to consider the past as the past when he has elements in the present that could comfort his identity. Today an Arab feels like a stranger in the world. An Iranian also feels like a stranger. He has the impression of living in a world that does not belong to him. He has the impression of living in a world that belongs to others, and he is a sort of unwanted guest. And for me, the essential frustrations, the basic passéisme comes from this fact: one looks back to the past because one has nothing in the present to be proud of.

Sara Suleri

The idea of independence created a certain kind of complete hysteria in the subcontinent, then perhaps a connection with the idea of terror as it operates in the modern world. To go back to anxiety of the colonizer, however, that is a very different order of suffering because it is connected to reaping all the benefits of colonialism at the same time, but never stopping to recognize or acknowledge the psychic cost that goes along with the whole benefit of colonialism.

Julian Samuel

Can you particularize this psychic cost in a well-known figure, someone even more well known than Edmund Burke?

Sara Suleri

All right, let us take the classic example of Rudyard Kipling, the arch imperialist, the person who is able to talk about the white man's burden, to talk about issues such as East is

East, and West is West, and never the twain shall meet.

He was born in Lahore. He grew up being looked after by an *ayah,* and Urdu, or call it Hindi, was the only language that he really spoke until he was shipped off to England in order to go to boarding school. Kipling arrived as an eight year old child in Britain. He had never seen a fire in a fireplace before. He had to learn a different language and he longed for home.

Now that's one of the psychic costs of colonialism in that, even though the colonizers were meant to live as ideal English families, they were there, in this highly artificial world meant to recreate little Englands through out India, and they shipped off their kids to make little British gentlemens of them. And the children never really recovered from that kind of cultural trauma, even when they returned, as did Kipling. And you see that as a very strong influence in his writing and in his life.

M. Nourbese Philip

Livingstone is very illustrative of this kind of colonial: he has written that if he was given a choice to live in Scotland or to live in Africa with

Africans, he would choose to live with Africans. Of course, you would later find him being critical of them, but he also observed, for instance, that the more contact Africans had with Europe, the more degenerate he found them, as compared with those Africans who had very little or no contact with Europeans. Its all there in his words.

Livingstone was very clear about what was valuable in African civilization and culture. I have tremendous respect for him when I read of what this man did: walking across a continent and back, but we have to put that in perspective. It had been done before, several times by Africans and even by other Europeans, for instance, the Portuguese whom he then dismissed as being half-castes.

To get back to your former question about history, you see, this is why it is very interesting and important to read many of these people: the Columbuses, the Livingstones and so on. We know them for what they are. But it is often within those very texts that we find gems of information about our peoples that later on were destroyed.

Ackbar Abbas

I believe that what is happening in Hong Kong now is something that is unique in the history of colonialism and postcolonialism. What is different about the situation in Hong Kong now, and the situation in India in '47, is that Hong Kong is going to arrive at what you might call a postcolonial situation without going through the process of decolonization.

It is like the usual narrative: a process of colonization, decolonization, and then the post-colonial is a bit garbled here for the simple reason that when Hong Kong returns to China, you are not going to see the demise of capitalism and imperialism. I think that only the very naive would still believe that. What you're going to have is a transition from Hong Kong being under one colonial power to Hong Kong being under a very different colonial power, but a colonial power nevertheless.

But there is a kind of historical twist to this: when 1997 comes, Hong Kong at one level will be subordinate and dependent on China. At another level, it is very much advanced in terms of technology — in terms of its communication-al networks to international finance and so on — very much more advanced than China which would be the colonializing power. It is as if the colonized power is no longer in a subaltern, dependent, position on the colonializing power. For example, all the studies that the Subaltern Group did on India would not be so easily applicable to Hong Kong, simply because of these historical twists and paradoxes. It is a postcoloniality that in a sense precedes decolonialization: its a postcolonialism that has to take place before decolonization has taken place.

Thierry Hentsch

The problem is that anti-colonial criticism — or else the criticism against the neoimperialism or new forms of essentially economic domination — has not stopped, firstly, capitalist expansion, and secondly, it did not stop the elites in power today in the Third World — and even in those countries, purportedly progressive — from being, ultimately, currents of transmission of the capitalist trends in their own countries. Therefore, these critiques are dismissed and devalued today: one says, well, look, it did not work.

But of course it did not work because these critiques were never taken seriously, on either side, nor by the West nor the Orient. So, obviously, there is a grand deception on the part of Western intellectuals who see the governments, the elites, and even sometimes the intellectuals of the Third World who aren't abreast of the critiques of imperialism.

But the problem lies elsewhere. The problem is in the *rapport de force* which is extremely difficult to reverse for the Third World countries. It is a longterm work. It cannot be done over one or two decades. It is going to take centuries, probably.

M. Nourbese Philip

The traveller is in fact looking for Livingstone and she does eventually meet him at the end. They have a long and involved conversation about language and silence. She accuses him of being a silencer and so on. For instance, she says to him: "Do you remember those falls, the name of the falls?" And of course he says: "It was Victoria Falls." She says: "What was the name before that?" He, of course, does not know. And the traveller — this is the woman looking for Livingstone — tells him what the name was before, *Mosioatunya*, which means "the smoke that thunders." He is quite taken aback by this bit of information.

Ackbar Abbas,
critic

That was my way of showing, in a fairly obvious way, the silencing that went on by the European all around the world.

Thierry Hentsch

Some images say a lot. I talked about *The Raft of the Medusa*. What exactly is "The Raft?" It is a description of a miserable world facing the indifference of the rich. The raft is drifting, with starving people on it, desperately waving with whatever they have in their hands, their shirt, whatever, to signal their presence to a faraway boat which does not acknowledge, or even worse, does not even see them.

Julian Samuel

Is this the vision of CNN?

Thierry Hentsch

No. It could be viewed as a critique of CNN. In my opinion, *The Raft of the Medusa* by Géricault is a critique of the perspective that the West has of world misery, or else, a critique of a lack of perspective in the West.

The Raft of the Medusa is a critique of the indifference towards world misery which is also found within the Western World itself. It is my interpretation of the painting. I cannot help but see a prelude to the representation of the Third World, ignored by the West. Ignored and destroyed.

But it is obvious that other paintings are not at all as suggestive. Other paintings are merely the description of a way to perceive the world. *The Woman of Algiers* by Delacroix, which is a wonderful painting, probably offers a certain perspective on the status of women in Algeria. But it does not go beyond a vision of the Arab women shared by Westerners. It does not come near an illustration of the economic relations between the Arab Mediterranean and Europe.

Ackbar Abbas

When Hong Kong becomes part of China, then these two parts of the same country would be existing in different times and speeds.

I want to make a comment on the well-known formula that China came up with on taking back Hong Kong: "One country, two systems." It implies one country, which is China — and Hong Kong is part of China — and two systems, the socialist system, which would try to

THE MOORISH BATH
1870
JEAN-LÉON GÉRÔME

get along in the capitalist system that is operative in Hong Kong.

Amin Maalouf

I want to come back to the question of modernity. There have been two periods in the Arab world, in the Moslem world.

First, there was a period of expansion, of grandeur, during which the Arab world was one of the dominant forces, one of the dominant centres of culture in the world, on every level. I would say that this took place approximately between the seventh and eighth, and the twelfth and thirteenth centuries.

Then, there was a period of decadence that extends almost up to today.

At the same time, Europe experienced a period of great expansion, and from the fifteenth century, it became almost impossible to catch up with. For a long time the Arab world did not realize what had happened. The first shock took place at the time of Bonaparte's campaign in Egypt at the end of the eighteenth century. At that time, certain people saw that Europe had become something entirely different.

GENERAL BONAPARTE IN CAIRO, 1863
JEAN-LÉON GÉRÔME

shock took place at the time of Bonaparte's campaign in Egypt at the end of the 18th century.

There were two principle reactions. For some, it was absolutely necessary to catch up with Europe, and to do so, one had to imitate Europe in everything. The first to react in this way was Mohammed Ali in Egypt. He brought French counsellors, for the army, for all his ministers, for his minister of foreign affairs. There were others who had the same type of attitude, notably Ataturk, and the Shah of Iran to some extent.

There was another attitude which said the reverse: if we imitate Europe, we will lose our own identity. What must be done in fact, is to return to the period where we were dominant. That is, try to revive the conditions of the period of the seventh, eighth, tenth centuries, during which the Moslem world was the most important one, the most productive, with the most flourishing culture.

These two attitudes are always present: there are those who want to imitate, and those who want to go back to their origins.

The synthesis, in effect, is to be able to modernize without losing one's identity. And at this, the Arabs have not yet succeeded. If there is a country in the Orient which has perhaps succeeded somewhat in this, it is Japan. It has

THE RAFT OF THE MEDUSA

modernized itself, in some respects it has sur-
passed its Occidental model; at the same time
it has retained many elements of its original culture. Even so, many intellectuals in Japan consider that there was a betrayal of the traditional
culture — and I am not going to go into the
case of Mishima and others — but certain
people reacted in a very violent way towards
this modernization.

In the Arab world, in the Moslem world, we always have two poles that I will call, for the sake
of simplicity, the Khomeni pole and the Shah
pole. That is to say, the Shah of Iran wanted to
catch up with Italy in a space of fifteen years,
and Khomeni wanted to go back to the traditions of the seventh and eighth centuries. We
have never succeeded in solving this problem,
we are always divided. We have never succeeded in modernizing without losing our identity, and we have failed on both counts.

At times there are attempts at modernization,
but they are completely cut from the people. It
very quickly becomes the affair of a very small
Westernized elite. Because it is a minority, it
tries to impose this modernization by author-
itarian measures, by a kind of despotism, and
modernity becomes associated with the image
of a small despotic elite.

Or else we try to return to the past, we try to impose an Islamic economy, Islamic politics, Islamic war, and this does not at all correspond to the situation today. There again we end up with a failure.

Islamic culture is the culture people return to when they don't have a newer ideology they can refer to. Today, worldwide, there is an empty space, a crisis of ideology.

Previously, the Algerians imported, in some form, their ideologies from Europe. They imported a certain form of nationalism, they imported a certain kind of socialism. Today, what would they import from Europe? There is nothing. There is no ideology capable of mobilizing people in the world today. People in Algeria, as the people in Poland or elsewhere, return to what I would call the ideology by default, that is, the ideology that is present since birth, that they fed on with their mothers' milk: religious ideology. And their adhesion to this is the sign of a general crisis. This is the first element.

Another element: Islam as it manifests itself — as it manifested itself — in Algeria, in Iran, and in other countries, is fundamentally a form of Third Worldism. I see a lot of resemblance between the discourse of Khomeni and the discourse of Mao Tse Tung, for example. There are enormous resemblances. I would say there are even other resemblances between the Revolutionary Guards and the Red Guard. I do not think that the habit that we have today of considering a phenomenon such as Khomeni as a constant of history, is just. To my mind, Khomeni belongs to Third World history.

Peoples of the Third World are lost in the world today. They try to find a place, they have a tendency to demonise the West. When Khomeni speaks of the Great Satan, perhaps this is a term which makes you smile, but it is pretty close to expressions that could have been used by Mao Tse Tung or by Fidel Castro.

Sara Suleri

"Imperial binarism" is one of our favourite words in the academy these days. Essentially, it talks about binary opposites which have to do with the standard dichotomies, like good and evil, black and white, majority and minority, and understands the world only in relation to one thing versus its opposite.

Imperial binarism, which has to do with maintaining strict lines of demarcation between the colonizer and the colonized, is a mode that we

are trying to move away from. In such a mode, how many collusions can we count: collusions between the colonizer and colonized, collusions between struggles for independence and the British-bred notion of nationalism in India, and furthermore, collusions between the colonial period and the postcolonial period.

Ackbar Abbas

At the moment, China is going through a period of mourning for the socialist system, when in all important respects, it is becoming very much like Hong Kong. So what you are getting is one system at two different rates of development, or, if you like, two different speeds of development.

Rather, if you call the Hong Kong situation decadent — and I think I would call it decadent in a special sense — the progress is in fact the decline. It is not a period of progress followed by decline, but rather a certain kind of development, shall we say, one-dimensional development, which is itself a form of decline. So decadence is not a question of weakness, it could be, for example, an overdevelopment of a certain kind of strength.

Thierry Hentsch

What history really is, in other words, what really happened through history, will always remain unknown to us. Therefore, it is impossible to reconstruct the past as it was. But more than that: our attempts to partially rebuild the past through history is anchored in contemporary concerns.

History is, in a sense, a fiction designed to help us understand the present. Its mythical element becomes extremely important. But, careful, when I say "mythical," I do not mean "false." Myths do not oppose reality; they are part of it.

Let me give a concrete example: The Battle of Poitiers. In all European history books, especially French ones, we are taught that in 732, Charles Martel stopped the Arabs at Poitiers, and forced them back across the Pyrénées. This particular date became a crucial one for Westerners: this date constitutes the moment when we, Westerners, through our ancestor Charles Martel, stopped the Arabs.

But was it in fact a great battle? Not at all. The reports that we have show that this was not a particularly important one. Other battles followed after 732. It is not at all in 732 that the

Arabs stopped crossing the Pyrénées. There were several other incursions.

The reason why the Arabs stopped crossing the Pyrénées stems from internal disputes within the Emirate of Cordoba, and has very little to do with Charles Martel. But The Battle of Poitiers has become, from a mythical point of view, a crucial date in the history of the West, because the West gives a lot of importance to this particular date.

The mythical aspect surrounding the battle has nothing to do with reality. It plays a role which is extremely important in our imagination, which is to say, the way we perceive ourselves facing the Arabs.

The myth of The Battle of Poitiers says: "Here we stopped the Arabs, and from then on, we pushed back that frontier which separates 'us' from the 'other'." So mythically speaking, it is very important. It is clear that history is not simply reality. It means that the reality of history also includes what we think of it, and what we do with it. And what we do with it is largely mythical. Is this clear?

Amin Maalouf

For me, the notion of heresy is a positive one. And, I would add, the notion of apostasy is unacceptable.

I think that the condemnation to death of a man for his ideas, no matter how he expressed them, is unacceptable. But what is even worse, I would say, in the Rushdie affair, is that there were countries, Moslem countries, which came together at a summit and declared that an individual was an apostate. For me, this is something that is totally contrary to the very idea of a charter of human rights. I do not understand how the word "apostate" can be used. An apostate is someone who changes religions. It is a fundamental human right to decide one's be-liefs, and if we put that back into question, it means that the notion of human rights has no value.

I would add that my belief in the matter is that there is an extremely perverse vision of the notion of belonging. I think that for a very long time, and right up to today, it was thought that man had to belong to a culture, to a civilization, to a nation. And for me, it is the reverse: it is man who is the centre, and it is cultures which have to belong, and it is beliefs which have to

belong, and man has the right, and the responsibility to be the meeting place of several cultures, of several religions. I think that exclusive
belongings are a real tragedy and I refuse
them. I support the idea of multiple belongings,
I support the fact that man is the centre, must
be the meeting place, must be the only thing
that counts. It is not man who is at the service
of religion, it is religion which is at man's service. It is not man who must be at the service of
ideology, it is ideology which must be at man's
service. It is not man who is at the service of a
culture, cultures must be at the service of man.
For me, these are fundamental things.

Sara Suleri

One thing that we should start doing is completely giving up a rhetoric of "us" and "them." I
think that it is one of the most dangerous ways
of maintaining the binarism and maintaining an
inherent enmity, within the binarism. We should
also move away from strictly biological definitions of race or gender, and of notions of cultural difference.

By biological, I mean that it should not be
necessary that only a woman can speak for a
woman, only a subcontinental female writer can
address that experience, that only an African-

American female poet can write about what it means to be Black, to be a woman, to be a writer within the culture today. So that, if we attempt to not go multicultural, (I think that much of that stuff is bad, much of that stuff does not break binarism, but in fact enhances it), we will be able to point to two things simultaneously: the communality of our experience as well as the cultural difference.

Julian Samuel

Does the architecture of Hong Kong tell us about the politics of Hong Kong?

Ackbar Abbas

I think it does in a very mediated sort of way. I suppose that the most obvious example here, would be to take the two bank buildings, the two most famous buildings in Hong Kong, the Chinese Bank which is built by the American-Chinese architect I.M. Pei and the Hong Kong Shanghai Bank built by the British architect Norman Foster.

At one level, what you see in these two bank buildings is an opposition between, shall we say, East and West, between China and Britain. These are the two most famous buildings in

Central. But at another level, what we see about these two buildings is that they are part of an identifiable architectural style. It is not as though you have one building — the Chinese building — which could be responded to as Chinese, even though one of the things that Pei has done, with the Chinese bank building, is to build this modernistic building. At the same time, on the podium, he introduced certain very traditional Chinese motifs, giving it a kind of instant ethnicity.

But that does not change the fact that what you have here is in fact, one architectural style. So the way I would relate this to the politics, would be to go back to this phrase that was introduced earlier on; this idea of one country, two systems. What you are seeing in terms of the architecture, as well, is that such a formula can very easily be dismantled. What you are getting in terms of architectural style is simply one system, even though this one system can be used by different countries, as it were.

So you don't have one country, two systems basically. It is one system. You might call it a late capitalist system which is operative everywhere.

Thierry Hentsch

For a long period of time, we admitted that the Germanic-Barbarian invasions were the central element which led to drastic changes of the Mediterranean organization held by the Roman Empire.

For a long time, we did not pay much attention to the Middle East which was going its own way. For many centuries, we were taught in school that the crumbling of the Roman Empire in the Western part of the world, was a consequence of the Germanic-Barbarian invasions.

Then, this thesis was put in check. At least one historian, a Belgian named Pirenne, firmly sustained, during the 1930s, a different point of view, which has become, today, the dominant one. His argument was that the Germanic-Barbarian invasions could not really upset the Mediterranean order, because these Germanic-Barbarians were partially Romanized, having adopted for themselves many of Rome's institutions, namely Christian institutions. Therefore, the invasions did not introduce any radical rupture. The real rupture was brought about by Islam.

And why then, in 1930, all of a sudden, this concern about the rupture brought about by Islam? Because then, England and France had been trying really hard, for a decade and a half, to colonize and dominate the Arab world, without succeeding. England and France failed to introduce Western values and methods in this part of the world. They could feel something like a resistance. This Islam, which Hegel described as dead, left behind history, or else, beside history, the West discovered that it resisted. It lived and resisted.

Therefore, we discovered that the frontier still existed, and was strong. And then we needed to demonstrate that the great Mediterranean unity that the Romans have built — that we have built, so to speak, because we identify with the Romans — no longer existed. Why? Because of the Arab invasions in the seventh century.

It is to say that we have to look at what happened during the seventh century. It is not enough to go back two or three centuries when the Germanic-Barbarian invasions occurred. Why? Because we are concerned, during the thirties, with the resistance of the Arab world towards what is, in fact, a massive invasion of this world by the West.

books that I have read, from all my personal experience, and don't need a label that refers me

Amin Maalouf

The centre is man. You, me, we are all meeting places. I have the right to be, at the same time, Christian, Moslem, Jewish, Buddhist. I have the right to borrow from all religions, from all ideologies, from all the books that I read, from all my personal experience. And I don't need a label that refers me back to a religion, to a variant of a religion. This is my profound conviction.

I am not trying to proselytize with this. I am not trying to say this is the path that everyone has to take. But for me, it is certainly my path. I refuse to belong to a nation, even if this is something which makes you smile, because this is a period when people are uncertain of where they belong. People today want to say: I belong to this religion, I belong to that nation, I belong to that culture, and I reject this. I understand it, but I don't have much sympathy for this evolution. I find it extremely retrograde. I have a lot of respect for people who say, I claim many nationalities, many cultures. For me this is the future, even though we may pass through a period of regression today.

Thierry Hentsch

We can try to illustrate how history was used and rebuilt, through the writing of history, in order to justify a contemporary situation in our society.

History is always written in the light of contemporary political problems. It seems obvious to me. We can show it. That is what I try to do in my book *Imagining the Middle East.*[5]

I try to demonstrate how we end up using the history of our relations with the "other," and the way this "other" is depicted through our vision of history, to strengthen a self-image, the image that we have of ourselves, an image we want to keep intact, or enhance.

Julian Samuel

One last question. The tender question of Chirine. What is this allegory all about? Who is she and why does she vanish?

Amin Maalouf

I would say that the whole story of Chirine, and the manuscript, is a sort of allegory for what the

It means that history is always written in the light of present political problems.

Orient becomes when it is at once taken in hand, and misunderstood, by the Occident.

I would say that the Orient is a victim of two factors, itself and the Occident. And there is a fringe of people in the Orient, a fringe which I myself belong to, who want to see things evolve, but who always find themselves caught between the rise of fanaticism in their native religion, and the wall of incomprehension in the Occidental world. And I can feel this everyday. Everyday I have to ask myself, is it really necessary to speak up? Is it worth it to speak? Are people going to understand one day? And I often avoid speaking about Islam. I tell myself that there is such a climate of suspicion, of intellectual terror, that subtle ideas, conciliatory ideas have less and less place.

* * *

credits

produced, directed, and edited by	Julian Samuel
production unit	Concordia University – audio visual department
	Jocelyne Doray
	Abuali Farmanfarmaian
	Michel Giroux
	Jesh Singh Hanspal
	Tanya Mckinnon
research assistant	Tanya Mckinnon
translations and subtitles	Jocelyne Doray
	Natasha Pariaudeau
	Julian Samuel
thanks	Ackbar Abbas
	Thierry Hentsch
	Amin Maalouf
	M. Nourbese Philip
	Sara Suleri
	Charles Acland
	Begum Akhtar
	Koko Amarteifio
	Arab World Institute – L'Unité Audiovisuelle Mime Redjala
	Rana Bose
	Shawn Copeland
	Michael Dorland
	Mona Fahmy
	Vera Frenkel
	Sophie and François Gourmelon
	G. Grice
	Sean Kane

Abigail McCullough
Ian Mclachlan
Alix Parlour
Lelia Sebbar
Naushad Siddique
Marie-Blanche Tahon
Salima Vilinia

Stills   Panagiotis Pantazidis

Funding   The Canada Council

Illustrations of paintings
taken from   The Orientalists —
Michelle Verrier, 1979

Eastern Encounters,
Orientalists Painters of the
Nineteeth Century —
The Fine Art Society, 1978

The Orientalists: Delacroix
to *Matisse,* edited by
Mary-Anne Stevens, 1984

Islam and The Arab World,
edited Bernard Lewis, 1976
Archives, Washington, D.C

2.

ON AND
AROUND
THE RAFT

an interview with
Marwan Hassan

by Will Straw

ON AND AROUND THE RAFT

Marwan Hassan and Will Straw

Marwan Hassan is a writer of fiction and essays, living in Ottawa. We became acquainted as our paths crossed in the neighbourhood we shared and the bookstore in which he worked. Formerly, Marwan was a member of the collective which operated Octopus Books, a store whose role in nourishing an activist, oppositional politics in the national capital has been considerable. When asked to contribute an essay to this volume, I proposed instead that Marwan and I pursue a dialogue around issues raised in The Raft of the Medusa. *Over two afternoons, we talked in a rather open-ended way about questions of postcoloniality, intellectual work and the politics of culture. These conversations were taped and transcribed, and subsequently edited in a collaborative fashion* (**Will Straw**).

* * *

Will Straw: Let us begin by talking about the term "postcolonial." There are those who speak of countries such as Canada or Australia as being postcolonial, as if, in this respect, they share something with nations like India or Senegal. Is it legitimate to speak of Canada as a postcolonial country, or is this to dilute the term? And another question: Is the condition of postcoloniality specific only to those countries which were once colonized? Or could we say, as others have, that the term refers more broadly to the whole of the present-day world, in that we all live amidst migrating populations, cultural diaspora and so on. Which of these various ways of conceiving of the postcolonial does most justice to the term?

Marwan Hassan: Well, I think that the term is full of all sorts of implications, but it is an interesting one to bring up in the Canadian context. The utility that it has, and the categories to which it applies — in terms of culture, population, national status and so on — make it a complex one. If we were to take the totality of what we call Canada, of what the Québécois call Québec or the First Nations call the totality of the First Nations, we would see that what we call postcoloniality in the Canadian context is quite brittle. The term does not have quite the cohesiveness that it does in the context of Algeria, for example. There, it seems to apply much more coherently in the explicit historic sense of the word.

I would say, going against some mainstream conceptions of postcoloniality, that Canada and Québec have been, and are, colonized societies at one level, but, simultaneously, they are affiliated to imperialist societies and projects via the U.S.A. and Europe — what I might call encapsulating colonizations. This is true even of the Québécois, and I know that for many people this will seem disturbing. We cannot, nevertheless, situate the Québécois within the same trajectory as the Palestinians or Vietnamese or South Africans or Algerians, because the Québécois are not an autochthonous people. The question of colonialism has much to do with indigenous status. It is not always a question of historical priority or mere presence, but since colonialism does incorporate some notion of autochthonic status, we must ask ourselves, in a very specific way, who constitutes a postcolonial people. And I think we must work through a good deal of that before we can use the term in a meaningful way in the Canadian or Québécois contexts.

I don't think we have yet struggled enough either intellectually or politically to term Canada or Québec postcolonial. I really don't like terms such as "White niggers of America." Maybe Fanon should be reread or something. Ironically, indigenous nations clearly are struggling but have not yet achieved the historical rupture with the conquering peoples in the Americas — the English, French, Spanish, Portuguese and Dutch. In short, I think this term postcolonial is premature and just a little affiliated with another "post," postmodernism — maybe they are goalie posts. I can't accept it very comfortably in the context of South Africa or Palestine.

WS: Writers such as Étienne Balibar have written of the crucial role played by literature — along with the newspaper and other forms — in forging a national imaginary, in creating the sense of a common, circumscribed cultural heritage. Part of the implicit work of literature is to produce the sense of linguistic cohesion which is an important foundation of nationhood. Does literature still serve this function? Is it part of the coming-into-nationhood? Or has it become principally a means by which diasporic populations forge a sense of collective identity across national boundaries? If literature was once national, is there a way in which it is becoming more and more anti-national?

MH: That is difficult to answer. It raises the larger question of the affiliation between a language and a nationality. This affiliation is not always so clear-cut. For example — and to remain within our own national context — we have two nationalities which clearly contend here an Anglophone and Francophone. But the question arises, not only of those newly arrived to Canada, but of the First Nations as well. If we look, for example, at the constitutional relationship which the French and the English have with that entity called "Canada," we see that it very perversely occludes languages like Mohawk, Cree, and a whole series of other languages which are indigenous to Québec and Canada. In this respect, there is indeed a tremendous, historical rupture between the notion of nationality and that of language.

I'm not sure that language is ever able to sustain the position of founding a national entity. Even in the context of a country like France, Balibar's position is highly contentious. People don't realize that up until the time of Napoleon, it was highly problematic whether France could sustain its hegemony over all the outlying regions. In Arabic, people will tell you that the classical idiom does not establish the idiomatic norm of today. There is Maghrebian Arabic, which is more common in Morocco or Algeria, and you'll hear people say they speak "Lebanese," which doesn't exist as a separate language, but is, basically, a dialect of Arabic.

WS: But is there a written Arabic which will unite all those different populations?

MH: Here again, historical questions arise, and Arabic has not always been historically stable in its written form, despite the unifying mythology surrounding it by both insiders, Arabs and Muslims, and outsiders. As you go back and see the original scripts, they vary quite widely, going back to Yemen. Arabic stabilized for a long time under the hegemony of Islam, which was not a nation. But since the seventeenth and eighteenth centuries, and through the nineteenth with the Ottoman Empire, Arabic has changed dramatically. We could look, as well, at India and the role of Sanskrit. I was just reading an essay in *Subaltern Studies,* by Bernard Cohn, in which he speaks about the "command of language and the language of command." In the seventeenth and eighteenth centuries, the British were trying to seize control over the subcontinent through the use of Persian and Arabic. Hindi, or "Moors," or even Hindustani or "Indostani," as the vulgar languages were then called, were initially marginal to their task, because especially Persian and, to a lesser extent, Arabic, were the administrative languages of the Mughal empire. The English had identified that power structure. So the relationship of nationality to a particular language has, historically, always been dubious when questioned in detail.

Let's take the example of Latin, which everyone assumes to have been the principal language of the Roman Empire. Right in the centre of this Empire there was a Roman-era Arabic civilization. George Bowersock and other archaeologists of Palestine — "Roman-Arabia" — have documented this very well, showing the powerful Arab-Palestinian continuity which preceded the Roman Empire and Rome's conquest of Palestine and continued to function within the Latin culture of the Roman Empire. Whether we're talking about India or China or France or England, I don't believe there has ever been a national language which encompasses the entirety of the cultural and social landscape. Political fiat by the State does not simply create a national language despite even the general goodwill of the majority of the people of that society. By the way, some of the same myths surround the State of Israel and its relations to Hebrew, English and Arabic. I mean Hebrew was never a dead language to Asian and African Jews even if it was to Europeans. I think most people have existed within some sort of vectors of polyglotism, where they affiliate with two or more languages often quite comfortably. Only with English as the language of global media command is the illusion that other languages don't matter, but that's basically only the mono- and uni-lingual anglophone's vision of the world — or, maybe I should say, of the word.

WS: In considerations of the relationship between nationality and literature, the category of allegory is often privileged. In *The Raft of the Medusa,* Sara Suleri speaks of those literary works which are national allegories — works in which national histories are condensed within the fictional lives of literary characters. I would ask you, as a writer, this question: Are works of fiction in the contemporary world drawn almost inevitably towards the condition of allegory? Fredric Jameson had suggested this is true of virtually all works of so-called Third World literature. More generally, it might be said that when reading a literary work, we increasingly tend to confront it as written by a person who is white or black or brown, male or female, from this country or that. We quickly move to the assumption that what is being recounted stands for a broad, generalized experience typical of certain categories of social or cultural identity.

In this respect, the tendency to read literary works as allegorical has become widespread. Is this, for the writer, a positive burden, or is it necessarily restrictive?

MH: I should be honest. I don't have, and haven't had, much sympathy for allegory as a writer and reader, whether national allegory or otherwise. To begin with, the notion of allegory, as we can trace its emergence within religious thought, has always had its advocates and opponents. There are always individuals or classes who will resist the allegorical, because they see within it an ideological force that prevents people from seeing themselves as individuals within a culture. Allegory, as a literary concept, is a very tendentious one. If the critic pushes the work or the individual artist towards a representation of a culture which is allegorical, a whole series of questions arise, in particular, those having to do with class. One must always ask: Who is the author of allegory claiming to represent from within the collectivity of a culture? An example may illustrate this.

Let us take works generally considered to be allegories, such as Milton's *Paradise Lost* or Dante's *The Divine Comedy.* Northrop Frye would say that these are all linked to The Great Code, that of the Bible. But if you are standing outside that tradition, historically, then there is not the affiliation between writer and reader upon which allegory depends. Allegory is easier to sustain when this affiliation exists. But what happens, for example, when a Muslim reads *The Divine Comedy* and gets into the *Inferno?* The allegory cannot sustain itself, because this Muslim reader finds people like Salah-ad-din and Muhammad in Hell. The allegory of *The Divine Comedy* resonates forth a universal Christianity, and not every reader can accept that. By the way, I don't think it much sustains itself, even for the contemporary European.

From the point of view of a writer, I find allegory reductive. In a variety of ways, obviously, all modes of writing are reductive in some sense. Nevertheless, there are texts which give rise to — which invite — proliferating interpretations, or which suggest the contingent links between different classes and social forces. Allegory tends to reduce these contingencies and links, and therefore limits the range of possible interpretations, while seeming to be suggestive.

As a writer, I am not affiliated with a national culture in any immediate way. My first levels of identification have to do with class, and class resists. Class very powerfully resists allegory;

which is not to say that there are not elements expressive of class which may not be used allegorically. But it will be difficult to sustain these, because the first thing of which an affiliation with class makes you aware are the sorts of contradictions which allegory is not able to resolve.

WS: Could you be more specific about this literary affiliation with class? Is there not an ethnic component to your identifications as a writer?

MH: It would be totally false for me to say that one surface of my being is not bound up with being Canadian or Arab or, on a regional basis, a southwestern Ontarian. All of these are significant parts of my self, of my make-up. I can, nevertheless, say that my own political action and motivation has been conceived in terms of class. The difficulty has been that the Arabs, in a strange and perverse sort of way, constitute a class within Canada and transnationally. They've been compressed into one, in a perverse sort of way, even though they're not uniformly of one class. The Saudi millionaire is obviously not of the same class as the poor Palestinian *fellahin,* or Egyptian, or a child of Arab immigrant workers in North America. The difficulty is that the ideological construction of the Arabs in this historical epoch, as of the Jews, has formed them into what we might call a people-class, whether they like that or not. And, as a result, punitive relationships are imposed upon them from without.

My situation here is very contradictory because my own family's migration extends over a hundred years — beginning with my grandfather and continuing with my father and mother. It has been a physical migration, but, at the same time, a migration through classes. In one sense you could say, in strictly descriptive terms, that I'm a petty bourgeois. On the other hand, almost all my work experience has been working-class — either within the white-collar working class, as a clerk, or within the blue-collar working class, working for the railroad or as a janitor — very Canadian. Whatever class status my father and mother sought to achieve, in their transition from a peasant/Bedouin class to some sort of bourgeois status, they were not able to consolidate it, to guarantee it for me. The Anglo-Saxon mercantilist class, on the other hand, is normally able to guarantee this; once this status has been achieved and consolidated, it may be handed down in some form. On the other hand, there are members of my own family who have achieved this. Very clearly, then, I reflect certain contradictions. I identify first of all with class — and it's at the level of class that I seek to accommodate and grapple with a number of contradictions having to do with gender, sex, nationality, ethnicity and language.

I am an Anglophone Canadian; I can't write very fluently in Arabic. It would be pretentious of me to pretend that I could go back and recreate an Arabic identity as a writer. My status as a writer is somewhat contradictory because I am an Anglophone, but not of Anglo-Saxon culture, yet feel thoroughly knowledgeable about the details of Anglo-Saxon literature and its history. What's more, I have a deep and detailed … even intimate, emotional and profound knowledge of a particular region and geography of Canada, that is southwestern Ontario, which I find amusing that my fellow Canadians from other regions are quite dismissive of without exhibiting often even a simple knowledge of. This will cause howls of laughter, but if there is a physical place I miss, it is not so much Asia or the Mediterranean, but southwestern Ontario. I can't help this feeling, even if I'm not always comfortable with it socially. In one sense, I disagree somewhat with Maalouf. It is true, at one level, that you can select your existential relationships and identities, and say, for example, that you are a complex Mediterranean in sensibility. But what happens if there is resistance to your elaborating a more complex identity because that identity doesn't fit in?

After the Gulf War, a threshold was reached for me. The hatred was such that, even where I had not chosen to act as an Arab-Canadian, the sociological effect within Canadian culture was so unpleasant, so distasteful, that those people who were negating me were giving me definition. This occurred on such a broad social scale that I could not entirely resist a level of identification with Arabs, the disinherited, the wretched.

When, in the course of my political activity, I have engaged in other identifications of solidarity — with the Vietnamese or the Nicaraguans — no one reacted to me in this way. But when I was active *as an Arab-Canadian,* acting in solidarity with Palestinians or Iraqis, suddenly people came after me with hatred — hatred welled up within them, because my physical person could be immediately identified. At this threshold, I realized that Canada is a racist society. This is probably related to what Nourbese Philips talked about in the video. As a racist society, Canada won't relinquish some of these categories, not just for children of migrants from Asia such as myself, but for Blacks and Indigenous people.

WS: To return to the question of literary form, though, is there a way in which you can write from a subordinate class position and still elaborate something with a generalizing, allegorical force? Or will you necessarily end up writing what might be called counter-allegorical works?

MH: I can only speak of the novel, because that's what I know best. I do not think the novel can be immediately restricted to the perspective of a specific class, even if the novelist desires and wills that. Even when the novelist seeks an affiliation with the working class, wanting, as I myself do, to be of, with and for that class — even then, any novel must necessarily represent something of the amplitude of all classes. You cannot represent the working class through some narrow, highly specific "vulgar realism." A novel about elites, for example, could constitute a revelation as to how the working class behaves and performs.

A good example is that of Balzac, with whom Marx, of course, was fascinated. Another is someone like Robertson Davies. Robertson Davies could perform a great task for us. Culturally, economically and ideologically, he comes from an elite, whether he accepts that or not. It would be very interesting if he were to show us the inner workings of what is sometimes called the "Anglo-Saxon" elite in Canada. He has an intimate "insider" knowledge. But he doesn't take advantage of this. He embroils us in what are rhetorical strategies of character, plot and voice based on Jungian nonsense. Unlike Balzac, he doesn't perform the task of revealing to us the bourgeois classes as they exist in Canada.

What Marx admired in Balzac was not that he was an advocate of the working class — he wasn't — but that his works revealed the amplitude and dialectics of class relations at their subjective thresholds. It's on that level that fiction begins to provide subjective insights, which Marx knew to be very important — he knew that objective insights into culture, class and capitalism were very important, but he also knew that Balzac was performing a great task in exposing all the subjective relationships that characterized the bourgeois class and its formation.

WS: One of the first times we spoke to each other, I was browsing through the "Marxism" section of the store and mentioned, somewhat flippantly, that the only Marxism which interested me anymore was a vulgar Marxism. You mentioned your intention to write about the book industry in a way which focused on the largely unseen processes of labour and capital accumulation on which that industry depends. What interests you in these processes, and how do they effect the circulation of intellectual work?

MH: Our conversation, if I remember, had to do with the state of cultural studies, and with the refusal to look at political-economic questions even in discussions of shopping, for example. By performing a wide range of tasks in a bookstore, I believe I've learned a lot about the political economy of publishing, and I've become interested in writing about this.

To be honest with you, I find that these sorts of putative taxonomies or classification systems used in the analysis of culture are sort of caught in a terminological *cul-de-sac*. Popular or mass, low or highbrow culture — these terms don't describe much, even if they once may have done so. They come easily to mind, but they are insufficient to describe or name those things they are supposed to. Or, on the other hand, they provide a weak, coded language for talking around class without actually talking about it.

WS: There are really two absences in a lot of this work. In the first place, analyses of audience activity — of how people "read" texts in a variety of ways — block the question of whether things might be organized differently. At the same time, the new emphasis on ways in which particular social classes consume or "appropriate" popular culture obscures analysis of the very fundamental, material ways in which the labour on which this culture depends is organized. Based on your experience in what has been called the "book trade," what can you say about the conditions under which "intellectual labour" occurs?

MH: Here, I think, we can retrieve some elements of Gramsci's notion of the organic intellectual. I think this notion has become too simplified; we might add to it something of what Foucault has said about the interstices within which power takes shape.

Beneath the surface of the publishing industry is a whole layer of intellectuals — of doctors, engineers, lawyers and professors — who are not really seen as being part of the book industry, except insofar as they write the books.

Really, though, these are the organic intellectuals which the book industry requires. The reference works produced by these organic intellectuals possess the accumulated knowledge and accumulated capital which cannot be abandoned by capitalism. It is through these books themselves, as they are produced, bought and sold, that capital is accumulated within the publishing industry. Doctors buy each other's books, as do lawyers and other professionals. Their links to the publishing industry are much more intimate than in other areas of publishing, such as Harlequin Romances, where the people who produce books are not those who consume them.

What interests me is the way in which capital is able to incorporate certain kinds of intellectuals within it, so that they become truly organic in their relationship to capital. Let's take the example of engineers. Engineers evolved from the shop floor — they were, initially, working-class in every sense. They were mechanics, tool and die makers and so on. Capitalists observed the importance of these people and their intellectual work within the manual, industrial process. They controlled a body of knowledge which was essential to industrial production — an episteme, in a sense — and possessed the power to bring production to a halt. And so, in the nineteenth century, we saw a coherent development whereby the interests of capital professionalized the engineers, removed them from the shop floor, and made their knowledge seem the production of an academic environment. I see this as a tragic development. An important group which the working class had produced through its own energies lost its organic relationship to that class.

I can well see why someone might say to me "Look, you're a writer. That's a profession. What it's got to do with the working class?" My response would be not to simplify the predicament of class affiliation, but, rather, to dig at all the contradictions. I'm not sure whether this is a self-reflective question entirely, or a social question. The question could equally come up with respect to Julian, as a vidoemaker, and his video.

WS: The video is obviously dealing with the question of migration in its broad, generalizing sense, but one is invited, at the same time, to speculate about Julian's individual history and the place of that history in the conception of the video. After seeing *The Raft of the Medusa,* you suggested that the video seemed to replicate, in a compressed time frame, Julian Samuel's own migration to Canada, a migration which crossed more than one generation and several countries. It is not a video about returning to roots, but the process of directing the video — of undertaking a particular journey — reenacts a movement of migration just as it speaks of migration in a broader historical and theoretical sense. At the same time, it is not a video which has much to say about Canada or Québec. Is there, nevertheless, a way in which *The Raft of the Medusa* struck you as Canadian?

MH: It's funny — the video takes me back to when I was in grade school, in London, Ontario, and we would troop down to the basement and watch National Film Board films. Or when we would sit and watch the CBC on television, because we only received one channel. And, in strong contrast to the U.S. television I would see when I visited relatives in the States, Canadian television was notable for a certain pacing. This, I know, has become a cliché about Canadian television, but I have always found this pacing curious. It is not a pace which tantalizes, or excites, or appeals, and I think people tend to identify it with a certain banality or boredom. However, as I get older and think back to that pacing, there is something which is non-violent, rhythmic and almost seasonal about it that I find appealing. I would say that part of the sensibility underlying the video is a very Canadian one — there is a pacing based on certain concepts of reason which are at a certain level, false, but at another level, true. It's not tantalizing, engaging, or exciting, and it lacks sensuous gratification, but neither does it exhaust in the way that a U.S. film [or video] does.

* * *

HYBRIDITY AND THE SUBVERSION OF FRONTIERS

THE VAMPIRE AND THE RAFT

by Charles Acland

HYBRIDITY AND THE SUBVERSION OF FRONTIERS: THE VAMPIRE AND THE RAFT[1]

Charles Acland

A decade ago, Homi Bhabha defined a colonial discourse as:

> … an apparatus that turns on the recognition and disavowal of racial/cultural/historical differences. Its predominant strategic function is the creation of a space for a 'subject peoples' through the production of knowledges in terms of which surveillance is exercised and a complex form of pleasure/unpleasure is incited … The objective of colonial discourse is to construe the colonized as a population of degenerate types on the basis of racial origin, in order to justify conquest and to establish systems of administration and instruction.[2]

Colonial discourse, as Bhabha put it, engages a series of counterpoised qualities and attributes such as recognition/disavowal, pleasure/unpleasure, surveyor/surveyed, and degenerate/civilized. The arrangement maps out the relations of power in the broader scheme of colonizer and colonized. More than the politics of metaphor or imagery, colonial discourse *produces* subjects, *enacts* power, and, does so "to justify conquest." In other words, having learned the lessons of Foucault, knowledge has material consequences; it initiates policy, sensibilities and structures of oppression and resistance.

However, Bhabha was careful to avoid making Orientalism into an us/them historical apparatus. Instead, he suggested, one needs to consider both the *fixity* and *ambivalence* of colonialist ideology. Indeed, he criticized Edward Said's "semiotic of 'Orientalist' power … as a unified racial, geographical, political and cultural zone of the world."[3] The emphasis upon binary fixity, as Bhabha saw it, meant that a certain complexity of the articulated relationship was lost. This is because, he wrote, "it is difficult to conceive of the process of subjectification as a placing *within* Orientalist or colonial discourse for the dominated subject without the dominant being strategically placed within it too."[4] To fully comprehend this "placement within discourse" requires sufficient discussion of how the life of an imagined West lives throughout the globe, and how an Orientalist construction is appropriated back and circulates in, for example, the Middle East.

Julian Samuel's *The Raft of the Medusa: Five Voices on Colonies, Nations and Histories* reflects these abiding tensions between fixity and ambivalence, between recognition and disavowal. Especially extraordinary is the breadth of evidence and analysis demonstrated by the participants. They illustrate well that Orientalism has no single dimension or essence, but instead is continually constructed and reinvested in different historical moments. Consequently, excavating the machinations of colonialism must capture the very dispersal of the concept as it moves and circulates in a variety of forms. To this end, *The Raft* displays an easy and thoughtful flow between the five critics, and between their discussion of historical events (the Partition of 1947, the crusades), contemporary actors (Shah of Iran, Ayatollah Khomeini), and the production of Orientalist texts (Rudyard Kipling, Dr. Livingstone, and, of course, Gericault's painting). To this I would like to add the discussion, albeit incomplete, of colonial discourse. I will link this to ideas about a new postcolonial subjectivity, as suggested in *The Raft* and to the relevance of these questions to the Canadian context. I have chosen the following text through which to explore these themes, if only because it is so obviously an Orientalist work and yet rarely discussed as such, and secondly, because of its enduring popular currency. The text is Bram Stoker's *Dracula*.[5]

The novel opens with Jonathan Harker on a train to Castle Dracula in order to arrange the Count's move to London. The long journey presents many strange sights to the young Harker. In the opening paragraph, he notes the expectation of this in his journal, writing that "the impression I had was that we were leaving the West and entering the East; the most Western of splendid bridges over the Danube, which is here of noble width and depth, took us among the traditions of Turkish rule."[6] He embellishes his journey away from the familiarity of upper-class England with observations about the heavy use of paprika in food, the forbidding terrain, and the inhabitants' unusual manners of dress, who, "on the stage … would be set down at once as some old Oriental band of brigands."[7] Concerning a declining interest in the running of public affairs, Harker comments, "it seems to me that the further East you go the more unpunctual are the trains. What ought they to be in China?"[8] Despite this petty complaint, Harker desires to experience, then return with some exotic delights; for instance, he wants recipes for the "national dishes."

The most significant narrative shifts in the novel involve the movement between East and West of their respective residents. And even in these early pages, there is already a hint of the dangers of moving away from the shapes and contours of Western Europe. The air of mystery created by Stoker rests largely upon the description of this travel as a transgression of invisible boundaries of cultural life. In effect, the theme of the journey is a telescope of cultural difference, accentuating both the thrills and hazards of cross-cultural encounter. Before his departure, Harker visits that key imperial institution for the organization of the known and the unknown, namely, the British Museum. Here, he finds information about Transylvania and the Carpathian mountains. However, he discovers that there is no map of the location of Castle Dracula.

Stoker, thus, establishes the terms of the horrors that will follow, and they are clearly rooted in a popular conception of the links between the Western gaze and the civilized, the limits of which coincide with those of the British Museum. Images of Castle Dracula's distance from London suggest a terrifying and sexualized encounter with the "other." Later, the frontiers are also crossed in the opposite direction, when that unknown element, in the mutating form of Dracula, travels from the margin to the centre in his move to England. Dracula brings crates of earth from his homeland with him, an act which implies that this relocation is so supremely unnatural that the elements must be reconfigured in order to accommodate it. In this brand of essential nationalism, British soil is so richly soaked with British life that an alien breed would (or should) simply perish on it. As attacks on the two central women characters, Lucy and Mina, and a series of murders around London ensues, Stoker introduces a "coalition force" to combat the border-transgressor. Joining the British characters is a Dutch scientist and an American.

With Francis Coppola's "faithful" interpretation in his film *Bram Stoker's Dracula* (1992), critical discussion seized upon the themes of contamination, particularly having to do with the exchange of blood fundamental to the Dracula myth. Following this, an interpretation of the story as an AIDS morality tale establishes its contemporary relevance, a conclusion that is difficult to dispute. This, however, pushes further from sight the discourse of race at the core of the tale, one that is more appropriate to Stoker's context and, arguably, still lies hidden and silenced in more recent retellings. Consider the sequence, one dealt with at length in the novel, in which Lucy is having her blood not only drained, but polluted by some unknown creature, one that is clearly not entirely human (and certainly not British). As a temporary remedy, the men that surround her, the "coalition force," offer up their own blood, which they transfuse into her weakened body. The image is a compelling one: in the interest of saving the often-noted beautiful Lucy, a succession of robust, Anglo-Saxon men, as Stoker describes them, combat the contaminating influence of the alien with their "good" blood. It is understood, as their scientific minds reason, their blood is healthy and homogeneous, despite their international make-up; after all, they come from the same stock, the same class, the same race. Additionally, the women are constructed as the battleground for this struggle of blood — indeed, this struggle of lineage — between two races of men. Dracula, the hideous seducer of Western women, from an unmapped region where Western culture and rationality do not apply, is, in the end, the culmination of Western fears of the mixing of cultures and ethnicities. Dracula is the archetypal immigrant.

The immigrant-as-vampire metaphor is amply present a century after the initial publication and popularity of Stoker's novel: "they" sap national strength, steal jobs, breed rapidly, intermarry, avoid census-takers, avoid paying taxes, feed off the welfare contributions of others, and generally insist on being different. A most recent example of this fear is the proposal (not yet acted upon) by the Canadian government to move responsibility for immigration to a new ministry of Public Security. It is as though immigrant peoples arrive with crates of soil from their respective places of origin. The alarm caused by the possibility of this foreign soil being scattered indiscriminantly over the national domain initiates forms of special policing. This is analagous to what Amin Maalouf describes in *The Raft* as the difference between heresy and apostasy. The former, which easily describes the Dracula figure's relation to images of immigration, or even the mythic figure of Medusa as the heretical woman, offers a position of critique that the latter does not. The distinction is that the heretic harbours the possibility of revealing the discourse of difference operating at the frontier; apostasy effectively administers those differences.

Especially relevant to the critique of Orientalism, the Dracula myth is not just about the construction of the colonial subject in relation to binaries. Following Bhabha's contention, this myth is also about ambivalence, about the radial *mélange* and shifting constitutions of the boundaries between an imaginary East and West. In Stoker's *Dracula,* the area of contention is a near Orient, in what is presented as an ambiguous space at the Eastern edge of

Europe, against the known space of an American and European home. Put differently, perhaps the most peculiar, and most threatening, aspect of Dracula is that he is already part of "us." In a fairly enigmatic manner, Stoker reveals that taken-for-granted boundaries are in fact under contention. This can be seen as one instance of the formation of a "mobile colonial subject," with all of the same colonialist objectives of administering surveillance. Unlike the work of social Darwinists and the still recent memory of Gobineau which formed the context for Stoker's complex tale, today's racism operates on very different terms. In place of the distinctiveness of blood, we have what Étienne Balibar has called "neo-racism," where the operation of oppression of certain peoples deals with issues of cultural difference. Balibar argues that *"culture can also function like a nature,* and it can in particular function as a way of locking individuals and groups *a priori* into a genealogy, into a determination that is immutable and intangible in origin."[9] This has made immigration policy, with its process of evaluation based upon a discernible relationship between borders, cultures and peoples, a key site of subjugation and struggle. As Balibar notes, this will be accentuated since "the internationalization of social relations and of population movements within the framework of a system of nation-states will increasingly lead to a rethinking of the notion of frontier and to a redistributing of its modes of application."[10]

The interviews in *The Raft* display a serious engagement with the problems of writing from a mobile site. Cultural and postcolonial critique is complicated, and somewhat enabled, by the fact of writing from a home away from home: Maalouf, from Lebanon, now in Paris, commenting upon Iran; M. Nourbese Philip, from the Caribbean, now in Toronto, reconfiguring the travels of Dr. Livingstone; Thierry Hentsch, from Switzerland, now in Montréal, writing of the construction of *L'orient imaginaire;* Sara Suleri, from Pakistan, now in New Haven, Connecticut, providing critical analyses of British India; and Ackbar Abbas, discerning imperial tensions in architecture in Hong Kong, a colonial space where, as he comments, "there has never been 'a before'." *The Raft* presents five intellectuals working in five different locations. A strong argument emerges for speaking across and between borders, one which authorizes the necessity of providing critiques of entwining colonial discourses as opposed to speaking only of one's immediate situation. The continuum established by Samuel's editing structure is important, for it places side by side what has become an increasingly apparent and unfortunately banal experience of migration, and with it the mutability of what is meant by terms like "nation" and "ethnicity." Further, given that so many, worldwide, have lived in circumstances that have ultimately obliged them to leave places of origin (as immigrants, as refugees, etc.), the very idea of "home" needs to be revised to include the simultaneous making and unmaking of nations and identities. Instead of privileging homelessness, I submit that post-colonial criticism in part must offer some explanation of how places are constructed as homes, however provisional it may be. As Maalouf puts it, there is always a question of *appartenance,* of belonging. This does not always mean comfort and safety, but rather, belonging emphasizes an interest in the production of situatedness and mobility.

The question of "identity" has surfaced as a significant political issue, for this concerns the very basis of what one means by constituency, by community, by nation, in addition to how one sees oneself as an actor therein. Identity serves to empower notions of rights, access and speaking positions; in its best form, it encourages joy and celebration as well as the expression of evidence of discrimination and oppression. Traditional approaches to identity often asserted the need for unity and singularity. However, the breadth of appropriation and the general instability of a community's, any community's, sense of specificity complicate this now seemingly nostalgic vision, and point to the need for a rethinking of the relationship between identity and political action. As Stuart Hall describes it, cultural identity involves projects of continuity, of revealing "hidden histories," as well as projects of discontinuity, of difference.[11] Similarly, Ien Ang and David Morley write in their introduction to the "European Issue" of *Cultural Studies,* "we would like to stress the tensions between unity and diversity, forces of unification and forces of diversification, which in our view characterize life in Europe in the late 1980s."[12]

It has often been commented that backing away from the essentialist position has destroyed the certainty of a speaking position. This is because the nature of conditional, or conjunctural, politics implies that a critique cannot be guaranteed from one moment, or issue, to the next. Nonetheless, difference does not emerge from opposites that are fixed for ever and a day; it is relational, and depends upon an intricate array of components and features. It is never a thing in itself; it cannot be pointed to, nor prescribed. It does not float about like a trapped ghostly essence, waiting impatiently to be released. Difference can but exist in the historically contingent interrelationship between qualities, characteristics and activities. Saleri argues; the emphasis upon biological, that is, essential, definitions of difference dangerously works to reestablish the rhetoric of binaries. As she puts it, "it should not be necessary that only a woman can speak for a woman, only a subcontinental female writer can address that experience, that only an African-American female poet can write about what it means to be Black, to be a woman, to be a writer within the culture today." For this reason, the idea of the "hybrid" has gained a new theoretical currency.[13] Hybridity points to the complexities of ethnic and national identity. It demonstrates the non-essential nature of difference and national identity. The concept of hybridity presents itself as both a meeting, but not necessarily a smoothing, of historical contradiction *and* as an independent third term. It is that space of identity which negotiates those tensions between fixity and ambivalence, between continuity and discontinuity.

While it is used to describe virtually every form of national and ethnic identity, hybridity has evolved as a description of New World histories of migrating populations. Canada's status as a First World postcolonial nation denotes its own fraught relationship with otherness, and points to the intricacy of its hybridity. The international understanding of this prompts an American film reviewer to comment that Srinivas

Krishna's *Masala* (1991) is "as un-Indian as it is un-Canadian (and, yet, a film that could have only been made by an Indian in Canada)."[14]

Canada is subsumed with a sense that its project of national identity is a failure; not infrequently, attempts to rectify the national embarrassment of "culturelessness" present themselves, of which Preston Manning's Reform Party is one example. But, of course, Canada has never been "empty." Instead, what has often been conceived of as an absence has really been *the lack of a single unified space of national cultural identity.* Anthony Wilden's resonant claim that we are Imaginary Canadians, living in the ambiguous space of Not-land,[15] should be taken as a fundamental myth of indeterminacy of Canadian life; as such it is also the most ideologically successful strategy to disguise systemic neo-racism. No matter how uncertain Canadian identity may be, the cry is often heard that some living here are more Canadian than others. The argument of Canada's "neutrality" is merely an alibi to bury a teeming undercurrent of racism and the power structures that support it. The lack of a unified space of national culture means that there are many hybrid identities, offering a variety of possibilities for redirection. But there is also a set of boundaries and rules to their formation.

Some of these structuring forces are fairly predictable; no one is especially surprised by an immigration policy that selects "appropriate" candidates for citizenship, as wretched a practice as it may be. Other forces are unpredictable. For instance, as Philip has chronicled well in her essay "The White Soul of Canada" about the *Into the Heart of Africa* exhibit at the Royal Ontario Museum, so-called critiques of the history of colonialism are to be struggled over.[16] That exhibit demonstrated how the trumpet of multiculturalism is an easy instrument to sound in defence of a misguided project; if there is a lesson to be gleaned from here it is that, simply put, official multiculturalism is not an open invitation. One is reminded of Chandra Mohanty's comment that a frequent consequence of the hegemony of Western feminism for Third World women has been to conclude that "they cannot represent themselves; they must be represented."[17] Returning to Bhabha's definition, it makes sense to suggest that the discourse of hybridity creates a new postcolonial subject, one with potential losses and advantages over other forms of colonial subjectivity.

In conclusion, Samuel's *The Raft* falls neatly into a tradition of un-Canadian Canadian texts, because it too demonstrates the limited explanatory power of binaries. And for this reason it is sure to ruffle up some people. But, importantly, *The Raft* moves to the fore the argument that postcoloniality is about the transportation of cultures and critiques. As such, identity springs as a sullied amalgam of past and continuing colonial encounters. Otherness has often been reduced to a simple us/them situation, whether it is male/female, Occident/ Orient, white/non-white. Among other things, the central misconception here is that power is afforded a rather comfortable and obvious location. I see this as the optimistic scenario; if you can predict the location of power, it is an easy target to attack. But, difference is systemic, and the flow of exchange is not linear, or uni-dimensional. Systems of difference involve the entitlement of the terms of cultural and colonial encounter — that is, who gets to do the borrowing, how this is engaged, and who, ultimately, benefits. The challenge then is to lay bare the exigencies of colonialist discourse, for instance, in the replaying of the Dracula myth as a fear of the immigrant, and its relationship to structures of power, identity and hybridity. *The Raft* confirms that while we may have been left with what Philip calls "site[s] of vast interruption of histories," one can still, as Ackbar Abbas says, "put a kind of spin on it."

* * *

NOTES

1. I would like to thank Julian Samuel for valuable comments on this essay.
2. Homi Bhabha (1993) "The Other Question ...," *Screen* 24.6, p.23.
3. Ibid. The Critique is of Edward Said (1978) *Orientalism,* Routledge, London.
4. Bhabha, pp. 24-25.
5. Bram Stoker (1983 [1897]) *Dracula,* Oxford University Press, Oxford.
6. Ibid., p. 1.
7. Ibid., p. 3.
8. Ibid., p. 2.
9. Étienne Balibar and Immanuel Wallerstein (1991 [1988]) *Race, Nation, Class: Ambiguous Identities,* Balibar translated by Chris Turner, Verso, New York, p. 22.
10. Ibid., p. 26
11. Stuart Hall (1989) "Cultural Identity and Cinematic Representation," *Framework* 36, pp. 68-81.
12. Ien Ang and David Morley (1989) "Mayonnaise Culture and Other European Follies," *Cultural Studies* 3.2, p. 134.
13. See, for instance, *New Formations* 18 (1992), special issue on hybridity.
14. J. Hoberman (1993) "Multi Culti," *The Village Voice,* March 30, p. 51.
15. Anthony Wilden (1980) *The Imaginary Canadian,* Pulp, Vancouver.
16. M. Nourbese Philip (1991) "The White Soul of Canada," *Third Text* 14, pp. 63-77.
17. Chandra Mohanty (1988) "Under Western Eyes: Feminist Scholarship and Colonial Discourses," *Feminist Review* 30, p. 82.

PUBLICATIONS BY AUTHORS IN THE TRANSCRIPT

Thierry Hentsch, *L'orient imaginaire,* Les éditions de Minuit, Paris, 1988. *Imagining the Middle East,* Black Rose Books, Montréal, 1992.

Amin Maalouf, *Le premier siècle après Béatrice,* Bernard Grasset, Paris, 1992.
— *La Jardin de Lumière,* Jean-Claude Lattès, Paris, 1991.
— *Smarcande,* Jean-Claude Lattès, Paris, 1988.
— *Léon L'Africain,* Jean-Claude Lattès, Paris, 1986.
— *Les croisades vues par les Arabes,* Jean-Claude Lattès, Paris, 1983. *Crusades Through Arab Eyes,* translated by Joh Rothchild, Shocken Books, New York, 1984.

Sara Suleri, *The Rhetoric of English India,* Chicago; University of Chicago Press, 1992.
— *Meatless Days,* University of Chicago Press, Chicago, 1989.

M. Nourbese Philip, *Frontiers,* Mercury Press, Stratford, 1993.
— *Looking For Livingstone,* Toronto, 1991.
— Harriet's Daughter, The Women's Press, Toronto, 1988;

Ackbar Abbas, *City at the End of Time,* Introduction to *Poems* by Leung Ping-kwan, translated by Gordon T. Osing, Hong Kong; Twilight Books Company in association with Department of Comparative Literature, University of Hong Kong, *Cultural Studies* No. 3, Hong Kong, 1992.
— edited and introduced, *The Provocation of Jean Baudrillard,* Twilight Books Company in association with Department of Comparative Literature, University of Hong Kong, Cultural Studies Working Papers No. 2, University of Hong Kong, 1990.

NOTES ON THE CONTRIBUTORS

Charles Acland is professor of Film Studies at Queen's University.

Will Straw is Associate Professor in the Graduate Program in Communications at McGill University. From 1984 to 1993 he taught in the Film Studies Program at Carleton University in Ottawa. He has published in *Cultural Studies, Popular Music* and a number of anthologies and is co-editor, with Jody Berland and Dave Tomas, of the forthcoming *Theory Rules: Papers from the Art and Theory Conference*.

Marwan Hassan is the author of *The Confusion of Stones: Two Novellas* and *The Memory Garden of Miguel Carranza* (both published by Cormorant Books). He lives in Ottawa and is presently working on *Words and Swords: An Anagram of Appropriation* and a long novel as yet untitled.

Jocleyne Doray is a writer and translator who lives and works in Montréal.

Julian Samuel is a documentary video producer and writer who lives and works in Montréal.

RETHINKING CAMELOT
JFK, the Vietnam War and US Political Culture
Noam Chomsky

A thorough analysis of John F. Kennedy's role in the U.S. invasion of Vietnam and a probing reflection on the elite political culture that allowed and encouraged the Cold War.

Noam Chomsky provides a sobering, well-researched, and provocative countervailing perspective ... calls into question an international cultural icon, John F. Kennedy, a shining presidential knight charging toward a renewed, vigorous, and forward looking America. This work may help North Americans gaze more deeply into the structures of power that touch and tether all US presidents and world leaders, and may help draw bolder lines between appearance and reality.
Hour Magazine

200 pages, index
Paperback ISBN: 1-895431-72-7   **$19.95**
Hardcover ISBN: 1-895431-73-5   **$38.95**

YEAR 501
The Conquest Continues
Noam Chomsky

...offers a savage critique of the new world order that former president George Bush hailed during his 1991 war against Iraq — and whose roots Chomsky traces to the European-led colonization of the world that began five centuries ago.
MacLean's Magazine

What's new in Year 501 *is the Cold War recast as a facet of [the] North-South conflict over resources, markets and profits....The content flows from these pages in exactly the manner it was poured in: with conviction, vigor and honest concern.*
Montreal Gazette

280 pages
Paperback ISBN: 1-895431-62-X   **$19.95**
Hardcover ISBN: 1-895431-63-8   **$38.95**

IMAGINING THE MIDDLE EAST
Thierry Hentsch

Translated by Fred A. Reed

Winner of the 1992 English-language Governor General's Literary Award for Translation

Thierry Hentsch examines how Western perceptions of the Middle East were formed and how we have used them as a rationalization for setting policies and determining actions.

Hentsch, a specialist in international relations at UQAM, presents an understanding of Europe and the European self....For readers who want to understand the world of plural identities and the tactics of "appropriation," this is a very rich and necessary book.
Montreal Gazette

218 pages, index
Paperback ISBN: 1-895431-12-3   **$19.95**
Hardcover ISBN: 1-895431-13-1   **$38.95**

FROM CAMP DAVID TO THE GULF
Negotiations, Language and Propaganda, and War
Adel Safty

Preface by Rachad Antonius

Safty offers a general introduction to the Palestinian-Israeli conflict, then continues with a detailed examination and penetrating analysis of Sadat's foreign policy decision-making, concentrating on what took place at Camp David in 1978. He examines the role of language, propaganda and media interpretation of the Palestinian question and, finally, the war against Iraq.

Naturally, it is controversial, but that is inherent in the subject matter. Safty makes his position clear, and does a careful and responsible job in backing it up. The most interesting part is based on Arabic sources that are not otherwise accessible.
Noam Chomsky

281 pages, index
Paperback ISBN: 1-895431-10-7   **$19.95**
Hardcover ISBN: 1-895431-11-5   **$38.95**

GERMANY EAST
Dissent and Opposition
Bruce Allen

revised edition

…documented thoroughly enough to satisfy the professional researcher, and is readable enough to allow general readers to see dissent for what it is: the inevitable uprising of a suffering people.
Books in Canada

…extremely timely and welcome.
Social Alternatives

191 pages, bibliography
Paperback ISBN: 0-921689-96-9 $18.95
Hardcover ISBN: 0-921689-97-7 $35.95

NATIONALISM AND THE NATIONAL QUESTION
Nicole Arnaud and Jacques Dofny

A relevant and revealing comparison of the "national question" in Québec and Occitaine, a region in France that is also seeking sovereignty.

A wide-ranging series of observations which is at the same time easy and satisfying to read…
Ottawa Journal

133 pages
Paperback ISBN: 0-919618-45-6 $9.95
Hardcover ISBN: 0-919618-46-4 $19.95

THE NEW WORLD ORDER AND THE THIRD WORLD
Dave Broad and Lori Foster, editors

The New World Order analyses the problems and possibilities for Third World revolutions within the historical context of U.S. imperialism. This work is an up-to-date, indispensable resource drawn from the experiences of internationally recognized authors.

In addition to the editors, contributors include Ed Herman, Thomas Bodenheimer, Robert Gould, Samir Amin, Susanne Jonas, Dave Close, and Doug Booker.

160 pages
Paperback ISBN: 1-895431-16-6 $19.95
Hardcover ISBN: 1-895431-17-4 $38.95